Jewish Migrant Forces Conquest of West Jerusalem in 1948 and East Jerusalem in 1967

A Historical and Current Review with Arabic Translation

Theft of Palestinian Properties in West and East Jerusalem by Jewish State

With Map and Photos

D1602692

Ibrahim Matar

NEWMAN SPRINGS PUBLISHING
320 Broad Street
Red Bank, NJ 07701

First originally published by Newman Springs Publishing 2022

ISBN 978-1-63692-990-3 (Paperback)
ISBN 978-1-63692-991-0 (Digital)

Printed in the United States of America

JEWISH MIGRANT FORCES CONQUEST OF WEST JERUSALEM IN 1948 AND EAST JERUSALEM IN 1967
A Historical and Current Review with Arabic Translation

In 1948, Palestinian villages and neighborhoods in West Jerusalem were depopulated and their properties seized under the pretext of absentee property. Jews replaced Palestinians and enriched themselves at the expense of the dispossessed.

In 1967, thousands of dunams were seized from their Palestinian owners under the illegal pretext of confiscation for a public purpose and were allocated for the exclusive use of Jewish residential settlements surrounding Palestinian neighborhoods in East Jerusalem. (Note: 1 dunam equals 1,000 square meters.)

To the thousands of Palestinian Christian and Muslim families from Jerusalem, dispossessed and impoverished by seizure of their homes, villages, commercial and residential properties, and real estate lands and replaced exclusively by Jews who are enriching themselves on stolen properties up till today; and also, to truth

You cannot hide the truth. You cannot rewrite the history of Jerusalem. Jewish seizure of Palestinian property must be condemned and exposed for the sake of future generations.

هذا الكتيب مهداة إلى الآلاف من العائلات المسيحية والمسلمة من القدس الذين سرقت ممتلكاتهم المكونة من قرى بأكملها وبيوت سكنية وعمارات تجارية وأراضي من قبل الدولة اليهودية وأدى ذلك إلى إفقارهم واستبدالهم حصرياً باليهود الذين زاد غناهم من الأملاك المسروقة لهذه العائلات.

كما أن هذا الكتيب يهدف الى ابراز الحقيقة إذ لا يمكن إخفاء الحقيقة ولا يمكن إعادة كتابة تاريخ القدس.

سرقة الممتلكات من قبل الدولة اليهودية يجب أن تدان والحقيقة تكشف من أجل الأجيال القادمة!

Acknowledgments

I wish to thank my family, Liliane, Eng. Ibrahim Jr., Dr. Eyad, their families and grandchildren, Melina, Iliana, Dominic, Sebastyan, and Sandryan, and friends and acquaintances who encouraged me to proceed with the preparation of this booklet. I realized that it is imperative for our older generation to record our recent history, especially the traumatic events of 1948 and 1967, for the benefit of future generations.

From the oral history of Marguerite Nakhleh Catan Farah (my mother-in-law), I learned about the ordeal of the families living in West Jerusalem in 1948 and the reasons why they made hasty decisions to leave for safer grounds. I also learned that many other families were forcibly evicted from their homes in a policy of ethnic cleansing adopted by the Jewish forces.

I thank Jumana Zahran from the Commercial Press in Jerusalem, who spent many hours preparing the design and setup of the booklet. Her contribution was invaluable in producing the format of the booklet in preparation for printing.

I also thank Garo who accompanied me on many trips, for taking professional photos of many of the houses and depopulated villages in West Jerusalem as well as the Jewish residential settlements in East Jerusalem. I also used a few photos of villas in West Jerusalem from the recently published book of Dr. Adnan Abdelrazek, *The Arab Architectural Renaissance in the Western Part of Occupied West Jerusalem*.

Finally, I appreciate the editing of the booklet by Maher Abou Khater, and my son, Dr. Eyad Matar, who took the time to review and edit the English version.

Ibrahim Matar
Jerusalem, 2018

INTRODUCTION

The year 2017 marked three milestones in the Jewish migrant invasion and conquest of historical Palestine from the Mediterranean Sea to the Jordan River—one hundred years to the Balfour Declaration and its implementation by thirty years of British colonial rule over Palestine, seventy years to the UN General Assembly Partition Plan of Palestine, and fifty years to the occupation of East Jerusalem, West Bank, and Gaza Strip.

Under the partition plan, Jerusalem was to be an international city under UN trusteeship. However, the Jewish forces moved to occupy West Jerusalem.

From January to July 1948, Jewish terrorist forces succeeded in terrorizing the civilian Palestinian population from their homes and property.

The most infamous of these terrorist acts was the blowing up of the Semiramis Hotel in the Qatamon district of West Jerusalem on the night of January 5–6, 1948. Twenty-four Palestinian civilians were killed, including seven members of the Christian family Aboussouan; Hubert Lorenzo, the twenty-three-year-old son of the proprietor; and Spanish vice-consul Manuel Salazar Allende. This act was followed on April 9 by the well-known massacre of some 200 civilians, including women and children, in the village of Deir Yassin on the outskirts of Jerusalem.

As a consequence, many of the civilian families (including my family) left their homes to safer areas, mainly to the Old City of Jerusalem, believing that after the fighting is over, they will be able to return to their homes. Unfortunately, on May 15, the Jews unilaterally declared their state and did not allow any Palestinians to return to their homes and property.

Subsequently, the Jewish State proceeded to steal the private properties left behind by declaring the civilian population as absentees. Then came the occupation of East Jerusalem in 1967 and the dispossession of thousands of dunams of private property for the exclusive use of the Jews.

Finally, US President Trump declared recently that Jerusalem is the capital of Israel and off the negotiating table. By this decision, he condones the theft of Palestinian property from both West and East Jerusalem.

The Trump administration further proceeded to cut its contribution to UNRWA. The US contribution over the years is only a small fraction of what the Jews owe to the Palestinian refugees (absentees) from Jerusalem and the rest of Palestine. In Jerusalem alone, the Jews owe the Palestinians, conservatively estimated, billions of dollars being the value of seized assets, capital gains from buying and selling Palestinian properties, and the income derived from such property over the past seventy years since its occupation of West Jerusalem.

The Jewish State also owes the Palestinian people over $500 billion in 1948 for the complete destruction of over 418 villages, turning Palestine into earth and constructing over the ruins 500 moshavim and kibbutzim.

To conclude, I sincerely believe that peace will only come when the Jewish State recognizes the theft of the Palestinian properties, apologizes, accepts to pay reparations, and return such properties to their original legal owners.

Contents

JEWISH MIGRANT FORCES CONQUEST OF WEST JERUSALEM IN 1948

Throughout its history, Jerusalem was a united city. From the seventh century up to May 1948, it was an Arab Palestinian city with open access to the faithful of the three monotheistic religions.

Jerusalem was a model of tolerance and coexistence administered over the years by a Palestinian municipality headed mainly by a Muslim mayor.

The events of 1948 and 1967 changed this picture when Jewish forces conquered Jerusalem. Its western and eastern parts came under sole Israeli control. As a consequence, the conquering forces engaged in uprooting and displacing the indigenous Christian and Muslim Palestinian population, supplanting them exclusively by Jewish immigrants and dispossessing them of and appropriating their property. The objective is the permanent liquidation of the centuries-old indigenous Palestinian presence in Jerusalem.

This booklet describes the two stages of the conquest of the Holy City. It will expound on the real estate usurped by Jews in both West and East Jerusalem and the methods used to dispossess Palestinians in order to replace them with Jewish immigrants.

A map will be displayed to show the border changes that have taken place since 1948, the growing Jewish control of the Holy City, and the Palestinian properties, including villages, urban neighborhoods, and real estate lands that have been seized and/or confiscated from 1948 to present.

The First Stage
Post–May 1948—the Uprooting of Palestinians from West Jerusalem

The traumatic events between April and July of 1948 turned into permanent exiles and refugees the sixty thousand Palestinians evicted from their homes, neighborhoods, and villages in what came to be known as "Jewish West Jerusalem." This civilian population was forced to leave their homes by a deliberate wave of terrorist attacks designed to ethnically cleanse the city of non-Jews.

The most infamous of these acts committed by Jewish terrorist organizations was the massacre on April 9, 1948, of civilians in the village of Deir Yassin on the outskirts of Jerusalem and the blowing up of the Semiramis Hotel in the Palestinian neighborhood of Qatamon.

In September 1948, Israel declared all the Palestinian Arab civilian population "permanent absentees" and did not allow them to return to their homes despite United Nations General Assembly Resolution 194 calling for their return. As a consequence, all their property was declared "absentee property" and placed under the authority of the so-called Israeli Custodian of Absentee Property. In 1950, the Absentee Property Law, signed by David Ben-Gurion, then in his capacity as minister of finance, allowed the confiscation of Palestinian property and gave the custodian full authority to sell it. This was the "law" that the Jews created to carry out ONE OF THE GREATEST PROPERTY THEFTS OF THE PAST CENTURY.

Noted author Moshe Smilansky wrote in *Haaretz* at the time: "Towns, villages and agricultural property were robbed without shame and lawless individuals from the masses as well as the intelligentsia enriched themselves from occupied property" (July 26, 1949).

Below is a brief description of the Palestinian neighborhoods in West Jerusalem and the suburb villages seized and depopulated in 1948, whose houses and lands were incorporated into West Jerusalem's municipal boundaries. (See map 1, page 62.)

Sample pictures of the villas and Palestinian villages shown are today occupied by Jews (for more details about Palestinian properties, review the book by Dr. Adnan Abdelrazek under the title *The Arab Architectural Renaissance in the Western Part of Occupied Jerusalem*).

PALESTINIAN DEPOPULATED VILLAGES
IN WEST JERUSALEM IN 1948

LIFTA

*Lifta and its extension, the hamlet of Sheikh Badr,
and all the surrounding agricultural lands to the
north of Jerusalem.* The village and its extension
hamlet, Sheikh Badr, were completely depopulated between April and July 1948, and all the
property that was left behind was taken over
by Jews. According to a 1945 census, property
ownership records show that 89 percent of the
land was Palestinian, 9 percent Jewish, and the
rest public, as shown hereunder:

Palestinian	7,780 dunams
Jewish	756 dunams
Public	207 dunams
Total	8,743 dunams

Today, some of the old homes of Lifta
remain abandoned or destroyed, but most of
the houses in the modern neighborhood of
Lifta extending to Jaffa Road and other areas
are occupied by Jews. The village high school is
now used as a Jewish religious site. A number
of hotels, such as the Sonesta and Crown Plaza,
are currently built on Lifta property. More significantly, most Israeli
ministry buildings, including the Ministry of Foreign Affairs and
the Ministry of Interior, and the Knesset are all built on properties
in Lifta and the hamlet of Sheikh Badr. In fact, the land on which
the Knesset was built belongs to the Palestinian Khalaf family, who
today live as "present absentees" in the Sheikh Jarrah quarter of East
Jerusalem. This family still holds the title deeds to the land.

A view of some of the old houses in Lifta.

169 Jaffa Road Extension of Lifta. The building, consisting of shops and apartments owned by Marguarite Nakhleh Catan Farah, was built in 1935. It was seized by the Jewish State in 1948 as absentee property. Recently Liliane Farah Matar, the daughter of Marguarite, attempted through the courts to retrieve the property now worth millions. The courts rejected the appeal on the pretext the Jewish State has confiscated the property under the pretext of absentee.

Elementary and middle school of Lifta. Today it is being used as a Jewish religious institution.

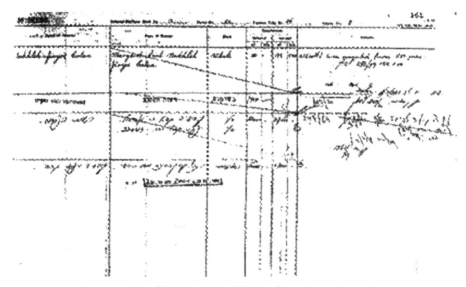

A case study of a Palestinian family from Jerusalem whose
property was usurped by the Custodian of Absentee Property.
The attached deed clarifies how the theft of property is effected.
This deed is issued by the office of deeds in Jerusalem.

In the first line, the deed records that Nakhleh Jiryas Catan sold
the property to his daughter, Marguret Bint Nakhleh Jiryes Catan,
for a specified amount.

The family of Marguret was living in their home in Upper
Baqaa of West Jerusalem. During the Jewish offensive in April 1948,
the security issue became critical for the family as Jewish forces began
shooting indiscriminately into the house.

Marguret and her husband, Dr. George Farah, and their four
children decided in April 1948 to leave their home and move to safer
areas in the Old City of Jerusalem.

In May 1948, the Jewish state was declared. All Palestinian
civilian families from Jerusalem who had moved to safer areas were
declared absentees and not allowed to return to their homes. The
Custodian of Absentee Property in the Israeli Ministry of Finance
takes over the property, and as such, the name of Margaret is crossed
out with a line as shown above.

In line two of the deed, the custodian sells the property to two Jews, Oweidi Gabay and Yafa Gabay, for the amount of PSP 17,500.

In line three, the name of the Gabays is crossed out as they sell the property to the inheritors of Moshe Barashi for the amount of £67,000. It seems that the property is still owned by the inheritors of Barashi.

This is the method that all villas, apartments, and businesses in West Jerusalem have, in effect, been stolen; and individual Jews enriched themselves while Palestinian owners were impoverished, living as absentees in exile.

The name "custodian" signifies that the property is in his custody for safekeeping and to be returned to the rightful owners. Unfortunately the function of this custodian is to steal the property and sell it to Jews only.

The Knesset in Jerusalem is built over the property owned by
Sheikh Ali Khalaf, one of the 2,500 inhabitants evicted by Jewish
forces from the village of Lifta and Sheikh Badr neighborhood on
outskirts of Jerusalem. In 1969, the newspaper *Yediot Ahronoth*
conducted an interview with Ali Khalaf who lived then in the
French Hill neighborhood of Jerusalem. He said, "The Knesset
is built on my property." He showed them the title deeds.

بنــي الكنيســت فــي القــدس علــى ممتلكات الشــيخ علــي خلـف أحـد ســكان لفتــا
وعددهــم 2500 نســمة طـردوا مـن قريــة لفتــا والشــيخ بـدر علــى مشـارف القـدس.

فــي عــام 1969 أجــرت صحيفــة يديعــوت أحرنــوت مقابلــة مــع علــي
خلـف الـذي عـاش بعـد ذلـك فـي حـي التلـة الفرنسـية فـي القـدس،
وقــال: إن الكنيســت مبنــي علــى أراضــيّ مبينــاً ذلـك بشــهادة الطابو.

DEIR YASSIN

Deir Yassin village to the northwest of Jerusalem. The whole village population was evicted as a result of a massacre of Palestinians perpetrated on April 9, 1948, by the terrorist organizations Irgun Zvai Leumi, led by Menachem Begin, and Lehi.

Land ownership records indicate that 95 percent of the land was Palestinian and the remaining 5 percent was Jewish.

(Percentages of landownership in Lifta, Deir Yassin, Ein Karem and el-Malha are taken from *Village Statistics, 1945* [Jerusalem: The Palestine Government, 1945].)

Palestinian	2,701 dunams
Jewish	153 dunams
Public	3 dunams
Total	2,857 dunams

Today, the Palestinian houses in the center of the village are used as a sanatorium by the Israeli Ministry of Health for the Jewish mentally ill. The village cemetery was bulldozed and paved over by a road leading to new Jewish residential settlements built on land belonging to Deir Yassin villagers. The stone quarries for which Deir Yassin was famous have now become a Jewish industrial zone. The village's two-room elementary school is now a center of the Chabad (Lubavitch) group of ultra-Orthodox Jews.

The road on the left of the picture is built over the destroyed cemetery.
The cemetery was bulldozed in the 1990s, witnessed by the author,
to build the road for the construction of Jewish settlements.

The village of Deir Yassin shown to the right of the picture.

Two-room elementary school of Deir Yassin today being used as center of Chabad (Lubavitch) group of ultra-Orthodox Jews.

The village of Deir Yassin surrounded by a fence is being used today as a sanatorium for Jewish mental patients operated by the Israeli Ministry of Health.

EIN KAREM

Ein Karem village to the west of Jerusalem.
The village was incorporated into the Jewish
West Jerusalem municipality as stated ear-
lier. The total Palestinian population was
evicted in July 1948. These were predominantly Christian Palestinians, as Ein Karem
is traditionally known as the birthplace of St.
John the Baptist. Land ownership records
show that Palestinians owned 90 percent of
village land and the Jews 9 percent; the rest
was public as follows:

Palestinian	13,440 dunams
Jewish	1,362 dunams
Public	218 dunams
Total	15,020 dunams

Today, the village is known as a Jewish
artists' colony, and its houses are inhabited
by Jews. The churches that still exist have
become museums, and although services are
held there, they lack their pre-1948 civilian
Palestinian Christian congregations.

Many Christian Palestinian families originate from this village
such as the Dibsi family who lived and owned many homes in the
village that are now inhabited by Jews.

Finally, it is one of the major ironies of history that Yad Vashem,
the memorial to the Jewish victims of the Holocaust, is built on
the terraced land of the dispossessed and exiled Palestinians of Ein
Karem. This memorial testifies to the fact that the Palestinians are
the last victims of Hitler, as they had to pay the price with their villages, lands, and country for the establishment of the Jewish state.

A view of the village of Ein Karem depopulated by Jewish forces
in July 1948. Today Jews live in the homes of the Palestinians who
were declared absentees by the Jewish State in September 1948.

More views of the village of Ein Karem now totally lived in by Jews who consider this village to be an artist colony.

Many churches exist in Ein Karem as it is considered the birthplace of John the Baptist. Unfortunately the churches are without congregations who have been dispossessed and today live as absentees in Bethlehem or in East Jerusalem.

EL-MALHA

El-Malha village southwest of Jerusalem. The whole Palestinian population was evicted in July 1948 and took refuge in the Bethlehem area. Ownership records indicate that 95 percent of the land was Palestinian and 5 percent Jewish as follows:

Palestinian	5,798 dunams
Jewish	922 dunams
Public	108 dunams
Total	6,828 dunams

Today, all the villagers' houses are inhabited by Jews. The new stadium and the Malha Mall, as well as some high-tech industries, are built on the real estate property of Malha village.

In summary, an area of close to thirty square kilometers belonging to the above-mentioned four villages that were occupied by the Jewish forces in 1948 had been built upon and today comprise most of the Jewish residential areas in West Jerusalem.

Over 93 percent of the land ownership of these four villages occupied by the Jews in 1948 were annexed to the West Jerusalem Municipality.

The value of these real estate lands exceeds billions of dollars, and these lands were stolen by the Custodian of Absentee Property and sold exclusively to Jewish developers and construction companies.

A view of the village of Malha showing the minaret of the
mosque built upon. This village had a population of seven
thousand Palestinians, all of whom were expelled in July
1948 and declared absentees by the Jewish State.

The Custodian of Absentee Property took over control of
the village and sold all the property exclusively to Jews.

More views of the village of Malha today inhabited totally by Jews.

Arab Residential Neighborhoods of West Jerusalem

Arab Residential Areas of West Jerusalem

In addition to the villages mentioned above, the Palestinian civilian population was also evicted from most of the residential quarters of urban West Jerusalem which came under Jewish control in 1948.

(See map 1, page 62.)

These Palestinian neighborhoods include the following:

1. Upper Baqaa Quarter (Waariyeh neighborhood)
2. Lower Baqaa Quarter (Greek Colony, German Colony, and el Dajaniyeh and al Namariyeh neighborhoods)
3. Qatamon
4. Talbieh
5. Mamillah
6. Musrara
7. Abu Tor and Jorat Al Annab

These residential neighborhoods consisting of thousands of apartments and modern private residences, villas, stores, offices, and family businesses were part of urban West Jerusalem, developed by the Palestinians outside the walls of the Old City at the turn of the twentieth century. Many Jewish families were living in some of these neighborhoods in apartments rented from Palestinian families.

Today all this property and houses are lived in by Jews in what they call "Arab houses." Many Palestinian houses were turned into Jewish religious schools or small private hospitals. In the Mamillah quarter, part of the Muslim cemetery was turned into the Israeli Independence Park, and these days, tombs of prominent Palestinian families are being destroyed—ironically—to make way for the building of a Jewish Museum of Tolerance on the site.

Additionally, the Jerusalem Theatre, owned by the waqf in Mamillah and previously used by the Israeli Ministry of Industry and Trade, is presently being destroyed to pave the way for the building of a new Waldorf Astoria Hotel.

Finally, the residence of Israel's president is built on Palestinian property in the formerly Palestinian quarter of Talbiyeh.

The present market value of the property belonging to the Palestinian inhabitants who were expelled in 1948 and are considered "absentees" and not allowed to regain their property in Jewish West Jerusalem is in the billions of US dollars. Thus, not only were the Palestinians uprooted, but they were also severely impoverished while the Jews enriched.

Abu Tor neighborhood was predominantly Palestinian in 1948. During the war, the neighborhood was divided: the Palestinians were able to retain the lower part of Abu Tor under Jordanian rule, and the rest came under Israeli control. The Palestinian properties lived in by Jews are located on the main road to Bethlehem. This is the reason that currently part of Abu Tor is Jewish and part is Palestinian.

Samples of stolen villas and residential buildings located in Upper and Lower Baqaa

The villa of the Kharoufeh family who now live
as absentees in the town of Beit Jala.

Three villas on the road to Bethlehem belong to three brothers from the Akra family—Costandi, Nakhleh, and George. They have been declared absentees and their villas sold by the custodian to Jewish owners.

The homes and shops belong to the family of Alwa'ri. This area is called Alwa'rieh neighborhood in upper Baqa'a of West Jerusalem. All this property was seized by the custodian of absentee property and sold to Jews.

The villa of Dr. George Farah built in 1945. The family lived
only three years before the house was taken over by the Custodian
of Absentee Property. In April 1948, the Farah family with four
children left their home, seeking safety as Jewish forces were shooting
indiscriminately into the house, endangering the lives of the children.

This villa was built in 1903 by Nakhleh Jeries Catan. This was
the first building built in upper Baqa'a. Nakhleh was from the
Orthodox Palestinian community and a well-known developer
and builder of houses in West Jerusalem. All his properties were
taken over by the custodian and sold to Jews. In his last days,
Nakhleh lived in exile in a house he owned in Jericho.

The home of the famous lawyer Henry Catan, the son of Nakhleh Catan. The wooden door is the same one that Henry installed in his house in the late 1930s. Henry ended up living in exile in France. His villa was seized by the Custodian of Absentee Property and sold to Jews.

The home of Engineer George Catan, also the son of Nakhleh. He was declared absentee in September 1948 and ended up in exile as city engineer of the town of Truckee in California.

A typical Palestinian home highlighting Arab architecture
built in the 1930s in Baqaa West Jerusalem.

The villa of Costandi Farah built in lower Baqa'a in the 1930s. Costandi
built the house with his savings working as auditor with the British
colonial rulers of Palestine. Costandi as all Palestinians, lost his home and
declared absentee by the Jewish State. He and his family lived in exile.

Palestinian home owned by the Dajani family
in the Al Dajanieh neighborhood.

Palestinian home also owned by the Dajani family.
Today it is used as a Jewish Synagogue.

Another Dajani family home. Agricultural Engineer Shehadeh Dajani was born and grew up in this house. He became a well-known agricultural researcher and lived the rest of his life in Jerusalem.

Samples of stolen villas and residential buildings located in Qatamon

The villa belongs to the Theodory family, declared as absentees. They lived in exile, impoverished in Bethlehem after 1948.

The villa of Ramadan family who were declared absentees and had their property seized by Custodian of Absentee Property.

What remained of the Semiramis Hotel in Qatamon district of West Jerusalem destroyed on the night of January 5–6, 1948. The explosion killed twenty-four Palestinian civilians including seven members of the Aboussouan family and Spanish vice-consul Manuel Salazar Allende. Today a Jewish family has taken over what remains of the hotel shown above.

Samples of stolen villas and residential buildings located in Talbiyeh

The villa of George Shiber, one of the founders of Talbiyeh quarter. His property was seized as absentee. He lived in exile the rest of his life.

The villa of Hanna Bisharat stolen and used by the Israeli Ministry of Foreign Affairs. It was used as residence by Golda Meir who declared that Palestinians do not exist.

The villa of Jallad family taken over by the Jews as absentee property.

The villa of Tarsha family in Talbiyah. The second floor is rented to the Polish consulate. As with the properties of all other families, this property has been taken over by the Custodian of Absentee Property.

The villa of Hanna Al-Tarsha built in the 1930s. The family was evicted in 1948 and lost the property. Despite that, today the family lives in the Old City of Jerusalem.

The villa of Dr. Tewfiq Kanaan, a well-known doctor who was called absentee and lost the property to the Custodian of Absentee Property.

Samples of stolen villas and residential buildings located in Mamillah

The Palace Hotel built in 1929 by the Islamic Waqf. It was the most modern hotel in the Near East. The building was taken over as absentee property and was used by the Israeli Ministry of Industry and Trade.

Samples of stolen villas and residential buildings located in Musrara

Houses in the Musrara quarter. Today they are totally inhabited by Jews. Among the many families who lost property is the Tleel family. Dr. John Tleel mentions his house in his book, *I am Jerusalem.*

SAMPLES OF PALESTINIAN COMMERCIAL PROPERTIES TAKEN OVER BY THE CUSTODIAN OF ABSENTEE PROPERTY IN 1948

The Sansour Building in the heart of the commercial center in Jaffa Road built by the Sansour family in 1935. The custodian took over the building and rented or sold many of these shops and offices to Jews. The Jewish State has made millions of dollars from this building while the owners, the Sansour family, have lost their investment and, as a result, were impoverished and today live as absentees in Bethlehem.

The Tanous Building on King George Street is a mixed-use residential and commercial building. The Custodian of Absentee Property took over this building; and as a result, the Tanous family lost their investment and currently live in Amman, Jordan, as absentees.

The middle building on Jaffa Road belongs to the late George Akra. He bought the building from another Palestinian family in 1945 for the amount of PSP 42,000. In 1948, the Akra family was considered absentee, and the Jews took over this building and have been earning millions in rent income since 1948.

List of Palestinian Owners Declared as Absentees

The following is a list of names of Palestinian families who owned villas, apartment houses, commercial centers, and buildings for rent in West Jerusalem urban neighborhoods. This list does not include thousands of families who owned houses in the villages around Jerusalem (Lifta, Deir Yassin, Ein Karem, Malha) that were incorporated by the Jewish authorities after 1948 to West Jerusalem.

All these families were declared absentees and their properties usurped by the Custodian of Absentee Property in the Israeli Ministry of Finance and sold or rented to Jews only.

The Jews have enriched themselves at the expense of the Palestinian families who were declared absentees, and many of them are present just across the border from West Jerusalem in East Jerusalem.

Below are the names of Palestinian owners listed by family name in each of the indicated quarters and neighborhoods in West Jerusalem.

Upper Baqaa Quarter

Batato, Albina, Qawwasm Meo, Lawrence, Abeelo, Qatran, Beiruti, Dawoodi, Abu Sabha, Sansour, Shammas, Jallad, Salim, Jahshan, Qattan, Al Malihi, Al Nammari, Al Qudsi, Al Malaabe Jallad, Al Wawi, Badinian, Musleh, Al Khuja, Al Tikhli, Dakrinian, Alyan, Mustafah, Jiddeh, Al Malli, Jubran, Khlaf, Abdelazziz, Dajani, Catan, Al Karam, Yasin, Gharbeye, Ghattas, Shinnawi, Faraj, Abdeen, Attallah, Akra, Attari, Francis Al Masaad, Al Sadir, Habash,

Dabdub, Ansari Dimian, Abu Alfeelat, Awidah, Attiyeh, Barakat, Al Baghil, Awad, Shaheen Istanbuli, Khateeb, Husseini.

Lower Baqaa Quarter

Salem, Barakat, Sammoor, Zakariyeh, Dahood, Darwish, Catan, Baghdadi, Nuzha, Maraqah, Hidawi, Farouqi, Al Sayegh, Dajani, Qutub, Abdo, Khashishayan, Abdel-Jah, Ramadan, Jaouni, Dawoudi, Ghannam, Al Haj Eid, Al-Rishik, Nakhleh, Al Keelani, Shahwan, Al Taweel, Obeid, Abu Harmah, Shammah, Haddad, Badriyeh, Albina, Sansour, Aqil, Shehadeh, Shalhab, Al Tammimi, Zeidan, Freij, Al Omari, Sarafeen, Abu Al-Feelat, Qreiytim, Kushaqji, Sarandah, Shehadeh, Anani, Al Deisi, Ejhah, Qbeise, Tanous, Tleel, Khouri, Al-Qutaa, Ghosheh, Marroum, Faraj, Deeb, Hananiya, Hallaq, Qamar, Al Tarsha, Nasri, Sabella, Jallad, Qawwas, Al Shiber, Al Ghouri, Bitar, Qarrah, Asaos.

Qatamon Quarter

Al Disim, Totah, Muna, Kalouti, Matooq, Freij, Dabbikeh, Kashishyan, Al Sakkab, Abdeen, Haineh, Kuttab, Abu Al-Felat, Albina, Qafiti, Tleel, Sakakini, Marcus, Al Mustaklib, Qawwas, Qamar, Al Dahoodi, Al Fityani, Oweida, Al Kalbuni, Ghannam, Haddad, Khouri, Sardisyan, Farah, Zatarah, Zankani, Yunis, Qleibo, Dedas, Karram, Kharufeh, Al Ama, Al Srouji, Al Mghar, Al Ghouri, Al Antari, Khamis, Said, Hindawi, Karkar, Nassir, Al Zaytuni, Al Massiwi, Husseini, Hassna, Ahram, Irani, Barakat, Al Tarsha, Marjerian, Kanaan, Harami, Bdour, Hababu, Al Taljeh, Dabbikeh, Al Ashmar, Niwaas, Abu Sabha, Al Massow, Sansour, Tadrus, Salloum, Aheninian, Lawrence, Nusseibeh, Sununo, Nassar, Afghani, Shaheen, Al Sous, Dimiani, Shamiyeh.

Greek Colony

Alfonse, Attalah, Abu Khalil, Ghneim, Yunan, Qawasmi, Stefan, Jiradis, Hazbun, Qura Zarzar, Kharufeh, Karkiyeh, Dajani, Assali, Qamar, Zakariyeh, Fattali, Mahshi, Sabbagh, Al Ouri, Qurt, Anastas, Al Kurdi, Tuniyeh, Munkian, Batshun, Abood, Salem, Nashashibi,

Barakat, Dabdoub, Halaby, Hananiya, Sayegh, Al Sayegh, Dimiani, Qabbani, Al Mamlook, Al Imam, Dadoosh, Fashi, al Shiber, Farran.

Nammariya Neighborhood

Al Nammari, Zawanah, Wahid, Khamis, Saniora, Al Shihabi, Al Sharkasi, Anqar, Barakat, Kevorkian, Kamleh, Khalili, Budeiri, Hammudeh, Al Bukhari, Al Dahoodi, Radwan, Khalaf, Tuqan, Al Hindi, Ayoubi, Al Saqa.

The Dajaniya Neighborhood

Al Dahoodi, Farun, Niman, Halaby, Abadi, Hamzah, Al Rayes, Al Disuqi, Al Arif, Al Borno, Al Dajani, Al Arabi, Al Kiswani, Al Jaouni, Abdo, Al Omawi, Tahbub, Al Nammari, Al Hazieni, Abu Al Saud, Deebeh, Hab, Abu Hammadeh, Al Assali, Shihab, Al Aori, Husseini, Jnadi, Al Khoureh, Jawaman, Asfoor, Tanous, Barakat, Al Julani, Faraun, Al Zughaiyer.

German Colony Neighborhood

Faraun, Habib, Khouri, Abu Ahmad, Mahshi, Al Nuno, El Imam, Lawrence, Dweik, Al Taziz, Al Tabbakhi, Haddad, Al Alami, Barakat, Badersiyan, Al Massow, Marjerian, Hammadeh, Dajani, Reesheh, Nimer, Al Assali, Al Jhaiyat, Al Dahoodi.

Upper Baqaa Wariyya Neighborhood

Al Deisi, Al Kalouti, Batta, al Nabulsi, Abdel Nabi, Hazbun, Anani, Abeed, Makhlouf, Attallah, Zkariyeh, Zaghrout, Marcus, Jallad, Kurdiyeh, Abu Meizer, Karram, Awad, Baltikian, Abu Mishal, Mazzal, Talamas, Handah, Qawwas, Al Syriani, Al Duzdar, Dimiani, Al Yazbem, Al Dwairi, Ehmairu, Al Amad, Farran, Dajani, Al Bandak, Abu Khalil, Siniora, Abu Rosah, Abu Judom, Shaheen, Arafeh, Qattan, Zawaneh, Salameh, Deeb, Nahleh, Mshahwar, Barakat, Shamiyeh, Taziz, Halaby, Nasrallah, Faraj, Al Arnaout, Al Jabari, Arnoos, Istanbuli, Nasser, Sabha, Husseini, Marta, Hab Ruman, Dabdoub, Sleiman, Al Wari, Karkirian, Al Amah, Totah, Zaghlul, Badriyeh, Dahbour, Natsheh, Abu Aiysh, Jabsheh, Salib,

Gheith, Al Daqaq, Hammudeh, Marjerian, Al Bitar, Al Assali, Judeh, Thakathedis.

Abu Tor (Elthory)

Barakat, Abu Khater, Al Tori, Al Sharawi, Wafa, Hidaiya, Abu Alfeelat, Al Qareen, Abu Ghazaleh, Itadiq, Al Hazineh, Nashahibi, Sultan, Zahran, Sheshan, Semonian, Awad, Haddad, Al Daoudi, Khader, Qattan, Abasi, Al Sharif, Abu Sarah, Alayan, Malaas, Ramadan, Razouk, Salamoni, Al Khalili, Al Haleemhe, Daghlas, Abu Gharbiyeh, Hashemee, Shamsiyeh, Abu Eitta, Al Munayer, Qleilat, Al Nabulsi, Bader, Al Shweikeh, Omran, Al Qaisi.

Talbieh

Salameh, Al Jamal, Bisharat, Tannous, Sununo, Dajani, Al Atrash, Murcus, Kanaad, Abu Shaqrah, Ohan, Al Kittani, Awad, Hallaq, Haddad, Andoni, Nasser, Hajjar, Ayoub, Sabbagh, Shiber, Mghanam, Khader, Karmi, Jalouk, Hagobian, Husseini, Jaqaman, Salloum, Habash.

Jorat Al Innab Neighborhood outside Jaffa Gate

Shawar, Rishik, Al Jaouni, Haj Asaad, Kamleh, Mohsen, Al Shurafa, Al Qawasmi, Al Nammari, Al Tahir, Mahdiyeh, Al Rifai, Abu Rmeihi, Bashiti, Abu Maizaer, Al Aejil, Zahideh, Nasser, Abu Gharbieyh, Himai, Dabbas, Qubty, Qurt, Al Hazineh, Barakat, Nashashibi, Diab, Nasser, Al Salti, Al Askari, Shamiyeh, Al Mani, Dadoush, Dahood, Sharaf.

Al Musrara Quarter

Haddad, Husseini, Al Syriani, Al Ansari, Al Alami, Halaby, Al Danaf, Al Mawqiot, Al Dajani, Al Khalidi, Al Tori, Musa, Jaaneeneh, Al Nammari, Al Disi, Zaatarah, Sbetan, Al Arif, Al Bashiti, Al Shwikeh, Al Shughuriyeh, Harami, Nashashibi, Thabit, Jaqaman, Aqil, Al Far, Mushahwar, Marcus, Saadeh, Deebeh, Jabsheh, Qattan, Najjar, Al Immam, Sharaf, Yasser, El Khouri, Sahhar, Hijaer, Musleh, Jwaliow, Allawi, Al Aarah, Khalaf, Esleem, Sider, Al Bahow, Mazhar, Al Kiswani, Al Abeed, Al Daoudi, Al Sharkasi, Al Duzdar,

Al Hakeem, Said, Ahmad, Al Bisyani, Al Mughrabi, Kurt, Al Faidi, Maraqah, Saba.

Source: Dr. Adnan Abdelrazek, "Chapter 6," in *The Arab Architectural Renaissance in the Western Part of Occupied Jerusalem*, 64–104.

JEWISH FORCES CONQUEST OF EAST JERUSALEM IN 1967

Jewish Forces Conquest of East Jerusalem in 1967

Post–June 1967: Annexation and Colonization of Arab Jerusalem

The second stage took place after the June 1967 Israeli invasion and occupation of Arab Jerusalem, which Israel came to designate as East Jerusalem, including the walled Old City. Shortly thereafter, the Jewish authorities embarked upon a series of measures to gain exclusive Jewish control over the city and to eradicate the Palestinian presence there.

The following is a brief account of the measures and policies adopted by the successive Israeli governments to Judaize the city and to solidify their hold over East Jerusalem. These ongoing actions clearly indicate that from day one of the occupation, the Jewish State never had the intention to withdraw from the Arab part of the city it had conquered:

1. *The dismissal and disbanding of the elected Palestinian municipality of East Jerusalem that had been functioning since 1948.* Ruhi al-Khatib (1914–1994) was the mayor of Al-Quds (East Jerusalem). Elected in 1957, his term came to an end on June 29, 1967, when Israel dissolved the city council of East Jerusalem following its conquest of the city in the Six-Day War.

2. *The formal annexation of Arab Jerusalem on June 22, 1967, by the extension to the city the law, jurisdiction, and administration of the State of Israel.* As a consequence, the city's Palestinian inhabitants were stripped of their rights as "citizens" and became known as "residents." This facilitated the procedures for the withdrawal of their right to live in the city should they travel abroad for business or any other purpose. As a consequence, some fourteen thousand Jerusalemites, born and raised in their home city,

have lost their residency rights since 1967. They can only enter the city as visitors.

3. *The demolition of over 135 homes in the Mughrabi (Moroccan) Quarter in the Old City to make way for the plaza next to the Western Wall.* As a result, some 650 Palestinians were left homeless. The process of eviction in the Old City continued, and some five thousand additional Palestinians were removed from their homes to make way for the expansion of the Jewish Quarter. Today, the Jewish Quarter has grown to four times its pre-1948 size. The eviction of Palestinians from their homes and the demolition of their houses continue unabated to this day in the Muslim Quarter of the Old City, in Silwan, and lately in Sheikh Jarrah.

The Mughrabi Quarter before its destruction in June 1967.

This picture shows the demolition of the Mughrabi Quarter in June 1967 to make way for the plaza in front of the Wailing Wall.

4. *The expansion of the municipal boundaries of annexed East Jerusalem to incorporate parts of the Ramallah and Bethlehem districts of the West Bank.* The drawing of the new boundaries is intended to maximize open land areas around Jerusalem and to minimize the number of Palestinians included within the new boundaries.

    As a result, the following villages, with a total population of eighty thousand were excluded: to the east are Hizma, Anata, Bethany, and Abu-Dis; to the west are Beit Iksa and Beit Hanina; and to the north are Dahiet al-Barid, A-Ram, and Qalandia refugee camp.

5. *The confiscation of Palestinian private property for the construction of exclusively Jewish residential fortress settlements within the expanded municipal boundaries of East Jerusalem.* These properties are seized in accordance with so-called Israeli laws and ordinances signed by the minister of finance under the pretext of "public purposes." The "public" refers exclusively to the Jewish inhabitants and the "purpose" is private residential apartments for them.

67

In contrast to the West Bank, land for the construction of Jewish settlements is seized under the guise of "state land" or for "security reason[s]." All these justifications for land seizure (or, to use better terminology, "theft" of Palestinian property) are illegal according to the Fourth Geneva Convention of 1948 (to which Israel is a signatory) and the Hague Convention of 1907 (the articles pertaining to occupied territories).

From 1967, a total of some 25,500 dunams, i.e., 25.5 square kilometers (1 dunam = 1,000 square meters), of private Palestinian real estate property have been expropriated as follows: (See the map on page 62 indicating the Jewish residential settlements around Palestinian neighborhoods.)

* *January and April 1968.* Five thousand dunams of land were seized for the construction of the first Jewish residential settlements inside Arab Jerusalem—the French Hill and Ramat Eshkol—as well as an industrial park in Qalandia.

* *August 1970.* An area of 12,500 dunams was seized for the construction of Ramot in the west (property belonging to villagers of Beit Iksa and Beit Hanina), Gilo in the south (property belonging to owners from Beit Jala, Bethlehem,

Beit Safafa, and Sharafat), Talpiot to the east (property belonging to Sur Baher), and Neve Yaacov in the north (property owned by Beit Hanina citizens).

Jewish settlement of Gilo built on lands confiscated from owners in Bethlehem, Beit Jala, Beit Safafa, and Sharafat.

Jewish residential settlement of Ramot, northwest of Jerusalem, built on confiscated lands.

* *March 1980.* An area of 4,500 dunams was seized for the construction of the residential settlement of Pisgat Ze'ev to the east (property belonging to owners from Beit Hanina and Hizma).

* *April 1991.* Two thousand dunams of land were seized for the construction of the residential settlement of Har Homa to the south (property owned by residents from Beit Sahur, Bethlehem, and Sur Baher). The purpose of this colony built on Jabal Abu-Ghneim is to allow for the construction of the separation wall to the south, separating Bethlehem from Jerusalem.

* *April 1992.* Two thousand dunams of land were seized for the construction of the residential settlement Ramat Shu'fat to the north (property owned by the inhabitants of Shu'fat) for religious Jews.

It is worth noting here that the construction of housing units on these expropriated Palestinian lands has not ceased since 1967. The Israeli authorities continue to approve more housing units for the expansion of each of the above settlements, such as the latest approval of an additional 1,600 units in the settlement north of Jerusalem.

6. *The transfer of Israel's government offices from West to East Jerusalem on seized Palestinian property.* Since the occupation, Israel has transferred the Ministry of Housing and Agriculture to the Sheikh Jarrah quarter in Arab Jerusalem. In the same quarter, the Israeli authorities have converted a government hospital built by Jordan pre-1967 into the Israeli Police Headquarters; and also nearby, they have built the headquarters of the Israeli Border Police.

* In another Sheikh Jarrah neighborhood, near the British Consulate General building, the Israeli Custodian of Absentee Property transferred (or sold illegally) to Jewish investors the house of the former mufti of Jerusalem, Haj Amin al-Husseini, for the construction of more housing units exclusively for Jews.
* On Salah Eddin Street, the Israeli government has transferred the civil courts to the courthouse used during the Jordanian period.
* High on a hilltop in Beit Hanina, the Israeli army has built the headquarters of the Israeli Central Command.
* In Ras al-Amud neighborhood, the Israeli government has transferred the police station which was built by the Jordanian authorities to Jewish investors to build more housing units for Jews.

7. *The construction of the separation wall that encircles the entire annexed part of Arab Jerusalem.* This wall, which is considered illegal by the International Court of Justice in The Hague, has created a large ghetto for the Palestinians in East Jerusalem and isolated them from the rest of the West Bank. Palestinians from surrounding towns and villages are not free to visit Jerusalem, which constitutes a serious drawback for the economic and institutional development of the city.

73

In the neighborhood of A-Ram to the north of Jerusalem, the wall separates Palestinians from Palestinians and defies the security pretext for the construction of this barrier. Furthermore, this wall has divided the West Bank into two parts and constitutes a major hurdle for territorial continuity between the north and the south.

The process of liquidating the indigenous Palestinian Arab presence has not ceased since 1948. The conquest and the Judaization of Arab Jerusalem continues through the destruction of Palestinian property, the dispossession and the eviction of Palestinian Christians and Muslims from their homes, and their replacement by Jews.

However, it is a known fact that all these Jewish schemes are not only illegal but also immoral and defy international legitimacy and Palestinian rights. Since 1967, all relevant UN Security Council resolutions have affirmed that Israel's policy and practices of settlement construction on occupied Palestinian land lacks any legal validity.

They have censured the annexation of East Jerusalem and have also called on Israel to rescind all measures that change the status of Jerusalem and to desist, in particular, from transferring parts of its own civilian population to the occupied Palestinian territories. . However, the international community has stood impotent in the face of Israel, unable to make it comply with these binding resolutions as was the case with Iraq or Iran. Israel continues to defy these resolutions, mainly due to the support of the United States and its veto in the UN Security Council.

The Israelis declare at every opportunity that their conquest of both West and East Jerusalem and the elimination of the Palestinian presence and the destruction of historic Palestine is now an accomplished fact and that "united Jerusalem" is the "eternal capital of Israel" and is not negotiable—meaning that all the uprooted Palestinians are not allowed to return and their seized property in Jerusalem has become Jewish forever.

The Palestinian negotiating teams made a big mistake to concede a priori West Jerusalem to the Jews and to call only for the end of the occupation of East (Arab) Jerusalem. All of Jerusalem should be on the negotiating table in accordance with the corpus separatum plan for Jerusalem put forth in the 1947 UN General Assembly Resolution 181.

For peace to be achieved in Jerusalem, Israel should undo the crimes it has committed against the indigenous Palestinian population and should be made to comply with the will of the international community and its resolutions. The failure to do so has only emboldened the Jewish State, the pampered state, to continue with its colonization and expansionist policies and its attempts at the liquidation of the Palestinian people and historic Palestine.

This article has shown that most of the land and stolen properties in West and East Jerusalem belong to the Palestinians who still hold the titles to these properties. The following map shows the Palestinian areas, villages, and neighborhoods taken over by the Jews in both East and West Jerusalem.

MAP 1
ANNEXED EAST
JERUSALEM

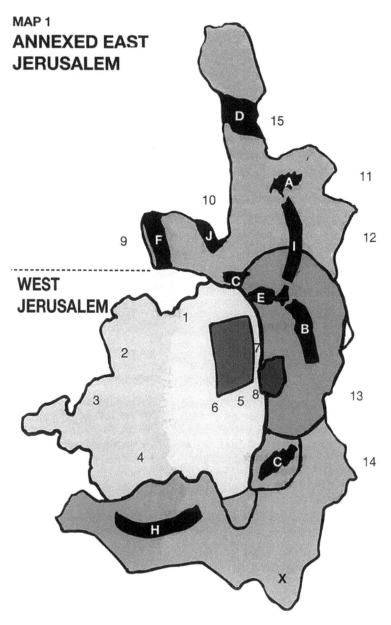

Source: I. Matar

Key to Shaded Areas on Map 1

 West Bank areas outside East Jerusalem municipal boundaries annexed to greater Jerusalem in 1967

 Exclusive Jewish residential fortresses built in annexed areas on confiscated private Palestinian land

 Only predominantly Jewish area in 1948 West Jerusalem

 Walled Old City of Jerusalem

 Palestinian area within East Jerusalem municipal boundaries annexed to greater Jerusalem in 1967

 Palestinian areas in West Jerusalem seized in 1948

Key to Letters and Figures on Map 1

Palestinian villages and urban Residential Areas in West Jerusalem taken over in 1948 still Occupied by Jews
1. Lilta-Khallet El-Tarha villages
2. Deir Yasin village
3. Ein Karam village
4. El-Maliha village
5. Talbiya Quarter
6. El-Qatamon–El-Baqɔah Quarter
7. Mamillah Quarter
8. Abu-Tor–Musrara Quarter

Palestinian villages whose lands were incorporated into Greater Jerusalem
9. Beil Iksa
10. Beit Hanina
11. Hizmeh
12. Anata
13. Bethany
14. Abu Dis
15. Ram

Post-1967 Israeli settlements in East Jerusalem and vicinity
First wave in 1968—1,200 acres seized
B. Mount Scopus (Hadassah Hospital and Hebrew University expanded from pre-1967 enclave)
C. Jewish and Mughrabi Quarters (expanded to four times the 1948 size; 2,300 Jewish settlers) Atarot Industrial Park (400-acre tract for Israeli industries)
D. French Hill, Ramat Eshkol, Ma'aleh Dafina, and Mt. Scopus (first Israeli housing colonies in East Jerusalem)

Second wave in 1970—3,100 acres seized
Neve Yaakov
F. Ramot (most developed of existing colonies with a population exceeding 40,000)
G. East Talpiot (built on private Palestinian land and in former UN zone; over 20,000 settlers)
H. Gilo (over 40,000 settlers)

Third wave in 1980—1,100 acres seized
I. Pisgat Ze'ev (40,000 Jewish colonizers; construction expanding to increase Jewish settlers to 50,000 by 2018)

Fourth wave in 1992—500 acres seized
X. There were 9,000 apartments approved in April 1995 for Har Homa, a new Jewish settlement. In May 1997, the Netanyahu government decided to begin construction. Today Har Homa is a big settler community of more than 25,000.

Fifth wave in 1992—500 acres seized
J. Ramat Shu'fat (3,000 units completed by the end of 1996; 20,000 Jewish settlers expected by the end of 2010)

Sixth wave in 1995—150 acres seized
Adding 7,000 units to the existing settlements of Pisgat Ze'ev and Ramot

UN SECURITY COUNCIL RESOLUTIONS ON JERUSALEM AND SETTLEMENTS

Resolution 242, November 22, 1967, affirms that "the establishment of a just and lasting peace…should include…withdrawal of Israel armed forces from territories occupied in the recent conflict."
Vote: unanimous

Resolution 252, May 21, 1968, was adopted in response to Knesset action extending Israeli law and jurisdiction over parts of the captured West Bank and Arab Jerusalem. The resolution calls on Israel "to rescind all measures to change the status of Jerusalem." The resolution notes "that all legislative and administrative measures and actions taken by Israel, including expropriation of land…are invalid."
Vote: 13–0, 2 abstentions (Canada and the United States)

Resolution 267, July 3, 1969, "censures in the strongest terms all measures taken to change the status of the City of Jerusalem." It calls upon Israel "once more" to refrain from all measures "which may tend to change the status" of the city.
Vote: unanimous

Resolution 271, September 15, 1969, reaffirms Resolutions 252 and 267 and "calls upon Israel scrupulously to observe the provisions of the Geneva Convention and international law governing military occupation."
Vote: 11–0, 4 abstentions (Colombia, Finland, Paraguay, and the United States)

Resolution 298, September 25, 1971, "confirms in the clearest possible terms that all legislative and administrative actions taken by Israel to change the status of the City of Jerusalem, including expropriation

79

of land and properties, transfer of population and legislation aimed at the incorporation of the occupied section, are totally invalid and cannot change the status."
Vote: 14–0, 1 abstention (Syria)

Resolution 446, March 22, 1979, "affirms once more" the applicability of the Geneva Convention "to the Arab territories occupied by Israel since 1967, including Jerusalem; determines that the policy and practices of Israel in establishing settlements...have no legal validity and constitute a serious obstacle to...achieving a comprehensive, just, and lasting peace;" and calls upon Israel "to rescind its previous measures and to desist from taking any action which would result in changing the legal status and geographical nature and materially affecting the demographic composition of the Arab territories occupied since 1967, including Jerusalem, and, in particular, not to transfer parts of its own population into the occupied Arab territories."
Vote: 12–0, 3 abstentions (Norway, United Kingdom, and United States)

Resolution 452, July 20, 1979, reaffirms that settlements "constitute a violation of the Geneva Convention relative to the Protection of Civilian Persons in Time of War" and "calls upon the Government and people of Israel to cease, on an urgent basis, the establishment, construction, and planning of settlements."
Vote: 14–0, 1 abstention (United States)

Resolution 465, March 1, 1980, reaffirms the applicability of the Geneva Convention to the occupied territories, including Jerusalem; "deplore[s]" official Israeli support for settlement; and "determines that all measures taken by Israel to change the physical character, demographic composition, institutional structure or status of the Palestinian and other Arab territories occupied since 1967...have no legal validity and that Israel's policy and practices of settling parts of its population and new immigrants in those territories constitute a flagrant violation of the Fourth Geneva Convention...and a serious obstruction to achieving a comprehensive, just, and lasting peace in the Middle East."

It "strongly deplores" pursuing these "policies and practices and calls upon the government and people of Israel to rescind those measures, to dismantle the existing settlements and in particular to cease, on an urgent basis, the establishment, construction, and planning of settlements...[and] calls upon all States not to provide Israel with any assistance to be used specifically in connection with settlements in the occupied territories."
Vote: unanimous

Resolution 476, June 30, 1980, restates the unlawfulness of Israel's annexation and transfer of its population to Jerusalem and reiterates that "such measures which have altered the geographic, demographic, and historical character and status of the Holy City of Jerusalem are null and void and must be rescinded."
Vote: 14–0, 1 abstention (United States)

Resolution 478, August 20, 1980, "censures in the strongest terms the enactment by Israel of the 'basic law' on Jerusalem and the refusal to comply with relevant Security Council resolutions; affirms that the basic law...constitutes a violation of international law and does not affect the continued application of the Geneva Convention... in the Palestinian and other Arab territories occupied since 1967, including Jerusalem;" and declares the recently enacted basic law "null and void."
Vote: 14–0, 1 abstention (United States)

Resolution 497, December 17, 1981, declares Israel's decision "to impose its laws, jurisdiction and administration in the occupied Syrian Golan Heights is null and void and without international legal effect;" demands that Israel annul the decision; and reaffirms the applicability of the Geneva Convention.
Vote: unanimous

Source: Foundation for Middle East Peace, bimonthly publication of the "Report on Israeli Settlement in the Occupied Territories" (Washington, DC).

هذا الجدار. وعلاوة على ذلك، فقد قسم هذا الجدار الضفة الغربية إلى قسمين كما يشكل عقبة كبيرة للتواصل الجغرافي بين الشمال والجنوب.

إن عملية تصفية وجود السكان الفلسطينيين الأصليين لم تتوقف منذ عام 1948. فيتواصل غزو وتهويد القدس العربية من خلال مواصلة تدمير الممتلكات الفلسطينية، ونزع الملكية وطرد الفلسطينيين المسيحيين والمسلمين من منازلهم والاستعاضة عنهم باليهود.

ومع ذلك، فمن المعروف كواقع أن جميع هذه المخططات اليهودية ليست غير قانونية وحسب ولكنها غير أخلاقية أيضاً وتُعد تحدي للشرعية الدولية وللحقوق الفلسطينية. منذ العام 1967، أكّدت جميع قرارات مجلس الأمن لأمم المتحدة المتعلقة بسياسة إسرائيل وممارساتها بأن بناء المستوطنات على الأراضي الفلسطينية المُحتلة يفتقر إلى أي شرعية قانونية. كما دعت هذه القرارات أيضاً إسرائيل إلى إلغاء جميع التدابير التي تُغير وضع القدس: كما دعتها الى الكف، على وجه الخصوص، عن نقل أجزاء من سكانها المدنيين إلى الأراضي الفلسطينية المُحتلة، كما أنها عارضت ضم القدس الشرقية. ومع ذلك، فان المجتمع الدولي يقف عاجزٌ عن مواجهة اسرائيل، وغير قادر على جعلها تمتثل لهذه القرارات الملزمة، كما كان الحال أيضاً مع العراق أو إيران. فتواصل إسرائيل تحدي هذه القرارات، ويرجع ذلك أساساً إلى دعم الولايات المتحدة والفيتو الأمريكي في مجلس الأمن للأمم المتحدة.

في كل مناسبة، يُعلن الإسرائيليون أن غزوهم للقدس الغربية والشرقية على حد سواء، والقضاء على الوجود الفلسطيني وتدمير فلسطين التاريخية قد أصبحت الآن أمراً واقعاً، وأن «القدس الموحّدة» هي <<عاصمة إسرائيل الابدية>> وأنها غير قابلة للتفاوض - وهذا يعني أنه لن يتم السماح لجميع الفلسطينيين المُهجّرين بالعودة وأن ممتلكاتهم التي تم مُصادرتها في القدس أصبحت يهودية إلى الأبد.

وقد قامت طواقم المفاوضات الفلسطينية بخطأ كبير بالتنازل مسبقاً عن القدس الغربية لليهود والدعوة فقط لإنهاء الإحتلال في القدس (الشرقية العربية.) ينبغي على القدس بكاملها أن تبقى على طاولة المفاوضات وفقاً لخطة الكوربوس سيبراتوم ((Corpus separatum) وتعني الجسم المنفصل باللغة الاتينية)) المتعلقة بالقدس والتي تم تقديمها في عام 1947 لقرار الجمعية العمومية للأمم المتحدة رقم 181.

ليتم تحقيق السلام في القدس، يجب على إسرائيل التراجع عن الجرائم التي ارتكبتها ضد السكان الفلسطينيين الأصليين وينبغي إجبارها على الامتثال إلى إرادة المجتمع الدولي وقراراته. وقد أدى التغاضي عن القيام بذلك فقط إلى زيادة تشجيع الدولة اليهودية، الدولة المُدلّلة، على مواصلة الإستعمار ومواصلة سياساتها التوسعية ومحاولاتها في تصفية الشعب الفلسطيني وفلسطين التاريخية.

وقد أظهرت هذه المقاله أن معظم الأراضي والممتلكات المسروقة في القدس الغربية والشرقية تنتمي إلى فلسطينيين لا يزالون يحملون أوراق ملكية هذه الممتلكات..

• نيسان أبريل من عام 1991: تم مصادرة ألفي 2000 دونم لبناء مستوطنة هار حوما السكنية إلى الجنوب (وتعود هذه الممتلكات لسكان من بيت ساحور وبيت لحم وصور باهر). والغرض من هذه المستعمرة المُقامة على جبل أبو غنيم هو السماح ببناء جدار الفصل إلى الجنوب، فاصلاً بذلك بيت لحم عن القدس.

• نيسان أبريل من عام 1992: تم مصادرة ألفي 2000 دونم لبناء مستوطنة رامات شعفاط السكنية إلى الشمال تعود الممتلكات لسكان شعفاط ليسكن بها اليهود المتدينين.

تجدُر الملاحظة هنا إلى أن بناء الوحدات السكنية على الأراضي الفلسطينية المُصادرة هذه لم تتوقف منذ عام 1967. وتقوم السلطات الإسرائيلية بمواصلة الموافقة على المزيد من الوحدات السكنية لتوسيع هذه المستوطنات المذكورة أعلاه، وأفضل مثال على ذلك هو الموافقة الحديثة على ألف وستمائة 1600 وحدة إضافية في مستوطنة تقع شمال القدس.

6. نقل مكاتب إسرائيل الحكومية من القدس الغربية إلى القدس الشرقية وذلك على ممتلكات فلسطينية مصادرة. منذ بداية الاحتلال، نقلت إسرائيل مكاتب وزارة الإسكان والزراعة إلى حي الشيخ جراح في القدس العربية. وفي الحي نفسه، قامت السلطات الإسرائيلية بتحويل مبنى مستشفى حكومي تم بناؤه من قبل السلطات الأردنية قبل عام 1967 إلى المقر الرئيسي للشرطة الإسرائيلية، وعلى مقربة من هذا المكان، قامت السلطات الإسرائيلية ببناء مقر شرطة الحدود الإسرائيلية أيضاً.

* وفي منطقة أخرى من حي الشيخ جراح تقع بالقرب من مبنى القنصلية البريطانية العامة، قام حارس أملاك الغائبين الإسرائيلي بعملية نقل (أو عملية بيع بصورة غير قانونية) منزل مفتي القدس السابق الحاج أمين الحسيني لمستثمرين يهود، وذلك بغية بناء المزيد من الوحدات السكنية التي سيسكنها اليهود حصرياً.

* وفي شارع صلاح الدين، قامت الحكومة الإسرائيلية بنقل المحاكم المدنية إلى المبنى الذي كان يستخدم كمحكمة خلال الفترة الأردنية.
وعلى قمة تلة عالية في بيت حنينا، قام الجيش الإسرائيلي ببناء المقر الرئيسي للقيادة المركزية الإسرائيلية.

* وفي حي رأس العامود، قامت الحكومة الإسرائيلية بنقل ملكية مركز الشرطة الذي تم بناؤه من قبل السلطات الأردنية إلى مستثمرين يهود لبناء المزيد من الوحدات سكنية لليهود.

7. بناء جدار الفصل الذي يطوّق كامل أجزاء القدس العربية التي تم ضمها. لقد قام هذا الجدار، والذي اعتبرتُه محكمة العدل الدولية في لاهاي غير قانونياً، بخلق «غيتو» كبير للفلسطينيين في القدس الشرقية كما قام بعزلهم عن بقية الضفة الغربية. ولا يملك الفلسطينيين من البلدات والقرى المحيطة حرية دخول وزيارة القدس، الأمر الذي يشكل عائقاً على التنمية الاقتصادية والمؤسسة للمدينة. وفي حي الرام إلى الشمال من القدس، يفصل جدار الفصل بين فلسطينيين من جهة وفلسطينيين من جهة أخرى وبذلك فهو يتحدى الذريعة الأمنية المزعومة لبناء

الأراضي المفتوحة حول القدس وبنفس الوقت لتقليل عدد السكان الفلسطينيين الموجودين ضمن الحدود الجديدة.

وكنتيجة لذلك، فقد تم استبعاد القرى التالية، والتي يبلغ مجموع عدد سكانها ثمانون ألفاً 80000 إلى الشرق – حزما وعناتا والعيزرية وأبو ديس إلى الغرب – بيت إكسا وبيت حنينا، إلى الشمال - ضاحية البريد والرام و مخيم قلنديا للاجئين.

5. مصادرة الأملاك الخاصة للفلسطينيين لبناء مستوطنات سكنية محصنة ويسكنها يهود بشكل حصري داخل حدود البلدية الموسعة للقدس الشرقية.

ويتم ضبط هذه الأملاك وفقاً لما يسمى بالقوانين والمراسيم الإسرائيلية الموقّعة من قبل وزير المالية، تحت ذريعة استخدامها لـ «أغراض عامة.» وفي هذا المصطلح، فان تعبير «العام» هنا يشير حصرياً إلى السكان اليهود وأما «الغرض» فهو إقامة شقق سكنية خاصة بهم.

وبعكس ما يجري في الضفة الغربية، ففي القدس الشرقية يتم الاستيلاء على الأراضي لبناء المستوطنات اليهودية تحت غطاء كونها «أراضي دولة» أو لـ «سبب أو أسباب أمنية.» كل هذه المبررات لمصادرة الأراضي أو، استخدام مصطلح أفضل، «سرقة» الممتلكات الفلسطينية غير قانونية وفقاً لاتفاقية جنيف الرابعة لعام 1948 (وإسرائيل هي إحدى الدول الموقعة عليها) واتفاقية لاهاي من عام 1907
[المواد المتعلقة بالأراضي المحتلة].

منذ العام 1967، تم مصادرة ما يقارب مجموعه خمس وعشرون ألف وخمسمائة 25500 دونم أي خمس وعشرون ونصف 25.5 كيلومتر مربع (الدونم وحدة قياس تعادل ألف متر مربع) من أملاك العقارات الفلسطينية الخاصة وذلك على النحو التالي:

• كانون ثاني يناير ونيسان أبريل من عام 1968: تم مصادرة خمسة آلاف 5000 دونم لبناء أولى المستوطنات السكنية اليهودية داخل القدس العربية: التلة الفرنسية ورامات اشكول، وكذلك المنطقة الصناعية في قلنديا.

• آب أغسطس من عام 1970: تم مصادرة إثنا عشر ألف وخمسمائة 12500 دونم لبناء حي راموت في الغرب (وتعود هذه الممتلكات لقرويين من بيت إكسا ومن بيت حنينا)، جيلو في الجنوب (أما هذه الممتلكات فتعود لمالكين من بيت جالا وبيت لحم وبيت صفافا والشرفات)، تلبيوت إلى الشرق (وتعود هذه الممتلكات لحي صور باهر)، ونفيه يعقوف في الشمال (ممتلكات تعود لمواطنين من بيت حنينا)

• آذار مارس من عام 1980: تم مصادرة أربعة آلاف وخمسمائة 4500 دونم لبناء مستوطنة سكنية في بسغات زئيف إلى الشرق (ممتلكات تعود لسكان من بيت حنينا وحزما).

84

المرحلة الثانية

مرحلة ما بعد حزيران 1967: ضم القدس العربية والاستيطان فيها

أما عن المرحلة الثانية فقد بدأت بعد الغزو الإسرائيلي في حزيران يونيو 1967 واحتلال القدس العربية والتي سمتها إسرائيل «القدس الشرقية» والتي تشمل البلدة القديمة المحاطة بسور. وبعد ذلك بوقت قصير، شرعت السلطات اليهودية بأخذ سلسلة من الإجراءات التي من شأنها فرض السيطرة اليهودية البحتة على المدينة والقضاء على الوجود الفلسطيني هناك.

وفيما يلي وصفاً موجزاً للتدابير والسياسات التي اعتمدتها الحكومات الإسرائيلية المتعاقبة لتهويد المدينة وترسيخ سيطرتها على القدس الشرقية. هذه الإجراءات التي لا تزال جارية حتى يومنا هذا، تُشير بوضوح إلى أن الدولة اليهودية، ومنذ أول يوم للاحتلال، لم تكن لديها النية أبداً من الإنسحاب من الجزء العربي من المدينة التي غزتها:

1. إقالة وتفكيك البلدية الفلسطينية المنتخبة في القدس الشرقية والتي كانت تؤدي مهامها منذ عام 1948. وفي أعقاب ذلك، تم إبعاد رئيس البلدية الفلسطيني المنتخب، روحي الخطيب، إلى الأردن.

2. ضم القدس العربية رسمياً في 22 حزيران يونيو من العام 1967، وذلك بواسطة فرض قانون ولاية لإدارة دولة إسرائيل على المدينة. ونتيجة لذلك، تم تجريد سكان المدينة الفلسطينيين من حقوقهم كـ «مواطنين» وأصبحوا يعرفون كـ «مقيمين». وقد سهلت هذه الإجراءات إمكانية سحب حقهم في العيش في المدينة منهم في حال سافروا إلى الخارج للعمل أو إلى غرض آخر. ونتيجة لذلك، فقد ما يقارب من 14000 مقدسي، كانوا قد ولدوا ونشئوا في مدينتهم الأم، حقوقهم بإقامة منذ عام 1967. ويمكنهم دخول المدينة كزوار فقط.

3. هدم أكثر من 135 منزل في حي المغاربة (الحي المغربي) في البلدة القديمة لإفساح الطريق لبناء ساحة مقابل الحائط الغربي (المعروف أيضاً بحائط المبكى أو حائط البراق) ونتيجة لذلك، تركت هذه العملية نحو ستمائة وخمسون (650) فلسطينياً بلا مأوى. وقد استمرت عملية الإخلاء في البلدة القديمة، وأُزيل ما يقارب خمسة آلاف (5000) فلسطيني إضافي من منازلهم لإفساح المجال لتوسيع الحي

اليهودي. وقد نمى الحي اليهودي ليصل اليوم إلى أربع مرات الحجم الذي كان عليه ما قبل عام 1948.

كما يتواصل طرد الفلسطينيين من منازلهم وهدم بيوتهم حتى يومنا هذا، ويتم ذلك دون هوادة وبنفس الوتيرة ويجري هذا في الحي الإسلامي من البلدة القديمة، في حي سلوان، وأيضاً، في الآونة الأخيرة، في حي الشيخ جراح.

4. توسيع حدود بلدية القدس الشرقية المضمومة إدخال أجزاء من محافظات رام الله وبيت لحم في الضفة الغربية. وتتم عملية رسم الحدود الجديدة بطريقة تهدف لضم أكبر قدر ممكن من مساحات

كانـت هـذه الأحيـاء السـكنية التـي تتكـون مـن آلاف مـن الشـقق والمسـاكن الخاصـة الحديثـة والفيلات والمتاجر والمكاتـب والشـركات العائليـة جـزءأ مـن القدس الغربيـة الحضريـة، التـي أسسها وطورهـا الفلسطينيين خـارج أسـوار البلـدة القديمـة فـي مطلـع القرن التاسـع عشـر. وكانـت تقطن العديد مـن العائـلات اليهوديـة التـي تعيـش فـي بعـض هـذه الأحيـاء فـي شـقق مستأجرة مـن العائـلات الفلسطينية.

يعيـش يهـود اليوم فـي هـذه المنازل والممتلكات فـي مـا يسمونه بـ<<البيـوت العربيـة >> كمـا تـم تحويـل العديد مـن المنـازل السـكنية إلـى مـدارس دينيـة يهوديـة أو إلـى مستشفيات خاصـة صغيرة. وفـي حـي ماميلا، تـم تحويـل جـزء مـن المقبرة الإسلامية إلـى حديقـة استقلال إسرائيلية ويجري فـي هـذه الأيـام، تدمير مقابـر العائـلات الفلسطينية العريقـة - ويـا للسـخرية - إفسـاح المجـال لبنـاء متحف التسـامح اليهودي علـى الموقـع.

بلإضافـة إلـى ذلـك، فـإن مسـرح القدس فـي ماميلا الـذي تمتلكـه الأوقـاف الإسـلامية، والـذي كان قبـل ذلـك وزارة الصناعـة والتجارة الإسرائيلية، يجـري تدميـره حاليـاً لتمهيـد الطريـق لبنـاء فنـدق جديد سـيطلق عليـه إسـم فنـدق <<والـدورف أسـتوريا.>> وأخيـراً، فقـد تـم بنـاء مقـر إقامـة الرئيـس الإسـرائيلي علـى ممتلكات فلسطينية فـي حـي الطالبيـة الـذي كان فلسطينياً فـي السـابق.

ويمكـن القـول بـأن القيمـة السـوقية الحاليـة لممتلكات السـكان الفلسطينيين الذيـن طُـردوا فـي عـام 1948 والـذي يُعتبـروا <<غائبيـن>> حاليـاً والممنوعيـن مـن استعادة ممتلكاتهـم فـي القدس الغربيـة اليهوديـة تقدر بعـدة مليـارات مـن
الـدولارات الأمريكيـة. وبذلـك، فـي الواقـع، فإنـه لـم يتـم فقط اقتـلاع الفلسـطينيين بـل وأيضـاً تـم قـد تـم سـلب ثرواتهم بشـكل حـاد.

الأحياء السكنية

بالإضافة إلى القرى المذكورة أعلاه، فقد تم أيضاً طرد السكان المدنيين الفلسطينيين من معظم الأحياء السكنية في المناطق الحضرية في القدس الغربية و التي وقعت تحت السيطرة اليهودية في عام 1948.
تشمل هذه الأحياء الفلسطينية ما يلي:

١. البقعة العليا و السفلى
٢. المُصرارة
٣. الطالبية
٤. ماميلا و الشماع

٥. جزء من أبو طور
٦. القطمون
٧. جزء من رحافيا

(ملاحظة: كان حي أبو طور فلسطينياً في معظمه في العام 1948 خلال الحرب، تم تقسيم الحي: فقد تمكّن الفلسطينيون من الحفاظ على الجزء الأسفل من أبو طور تحت الحكم الأردني، بينما وقع بقية الحي تحت السيطرة الإسرائيلية. والممتلكات العربية التي يقطن بها يهود تقع على الطريق الرئيسي المؤدي إلى بيت لحم. هذا هو السبب أن حالياً جزء من أبو طور يهودي وجزء فلسطيني).

اليـوم، جميـع منـازل القرويين مأهولـة مـن قِبـل اليهـود. وأمـا عـن الإستاد الرياضي الجديد والمركز التجاري المسمـى بمركز المالحة، فهي مبنية على أراضي تابعة لقرية المالحة وكذلك الحال بالنسبة لبعض الصناعات ذات التقنية العالية.

خلاصـة القـول: لقـد تـم البنـاء علـى مسـاحة مـا يـقـارب مـن ثلاثيـن (30) كيلومتـراً مربعـاً ينتمـون إلـى القـرى الأربـع المذكـورة أعـلاه والتـي تـم احتلالهـا مـن قِبـل القـوات اليهوديـة فـي عـام 1948، وتضـم هـذه الأراضـي اليـوم غالبية المناطـق السـكنية اليهوديـة فـي القـدس الغربيـة.

رابعاً: قرية المالحة

قرية المالحة جنوب غرب القدس.

تم طرد جميع السكان الفلسطينيين في تموز يوليو من عام 1948 ولجئوا عندها إلى منطقة بيت لحم. وكما تشير سجل المُلكية فان خمسة وتسعون بالمائة (95%) من الأراضي كانت فلسطينية وأن خمسة بالمائة(5%) منها كانت يهودية.

إحصائيات المالحة:

ملكية فلسطينية: 5798 دونم
ملكية يهوديـــة: 922 دونم
ملكية عامـــة :   108 دونم
المجمـــــوع: 6821 دونم

واليوم، تُعرف القرية على أنها مستعمرة للفنانين اليهود ومنازلها مأهولة من قبل اليهود. وقد أصبحت الكنائس التي لا تزال قائمة حتى اليوم متاحف وعلى الرغم من أنه يتم عقد خدمات كنائسية وقداديس هناك، فإنها تفتقر إلى طوائفها المدنية الفلسطينية المسيحية الوافدة للصلاة كما كان الأمر في ما قبل عام 1948.

أخيراً، إحدى الحقائق التي تُعتبر من المُفارقات الكبرى في التاريخ، هي أن «ياد فاشيم»، النصب التذكاري لضحايا المحرقة اليهودية ياد فاشيم تعني «يد إواسم» بالعبرية، قائمة اليوم على أراضي كانت مُدرجة وبها سلاسل تابعة لفلسطينيين تم طردهم من عين كارم والإستيلاء على أملاكهم. هذا النصب التذكاري يشهد على حقيقة أن الفلسطينيين هم آخر ضحايا هتلر لأنه كان عليهم أن يدفعوا الثمن بقراهم وأراضيهم وبلدهم لإنشاء الدولة اليهودية.

ثالثاً: قريـــة عيـن كـــارم

قرية عين كارم إلى الغرب من القدس:

كمـا ذكرنـا سـابقاً فقـد تـم إدمـاج القريـة إلـى بلديـة القـدس الغربيـة اليهوديـة. وقـد تـم طـرد جميـع
سـكان القريـة الفلسطينيين فـي تمـوز يوليـو مـن عـام 1948 وكان هـؤلاء السـكان فلسـطينيين مسيحيين فـي
أغلبهـم، لأن قريـة عيـن كـارم، كمـا هـو متعـارف عليـه بحسب التقاليـد، تحتـوي علـى موقـع مسقط رأس
القديـس يوحنـا المعمـدان. كمـا تـدُلُّ سـجلات مُلكيـة الأراضـي أن الفلسطينيين كانـوا يمتلكـون تسـعون بالمائـة
(90%) مـن أراضـي القريـة واليهـود تسـعة بالمائـة (9%)، أمـا بالنسـبة لبقيـة الأراضـي فكانـت أراضـي
عامـة.

<u>إحصائيات عين كارم:</u>
ملكية فلسطينية: 13440دونم
ملكية يهوديـة: 1362 دونم
ملكية عامـــة: 218 دونم
المجمـــوع   :   15029 دونم

و اليوم، يتم استخدام المنازل السكنية في وسط القرية من قبل وزارة الصحة الإسرائيلية كمصحة لليهود المصابين بأمراض عقلية . وقد تم تجريف مقبرة القرية كما تم تمهيد أكثر من طريق عليها تؤدي إإلى مستوطنات سكنية يهودية جديدة بنيت على أراضي تابعة لسكان قرية دير ياسين. وقد أصبحت مقالع الأحجار التي كانت دير ياسين تشتهر بها، أصبحت الآن منطقة صناعية يهودية. أما مدرسة القرية الابتدائية المكونة من غرفتين فقد أصبحت الآن مركزاً لمجموعة خاباد (لوبافيتشر) من اليهود المتدينين المتشددين.

ثانياً: قرية دير ياسين

قرية دير ياسين الواقعة إلى الشمال الغربي من القدس:

قد طُرد سكان القرية بأكملها كنتيجة للمجزرة التي تم ارتكابها في 9 نيسان أبريل مـن عـام 1948 مـن قِبـل المنظمـة الإرهابية المسماة إرغـون تسـفي ليئومـي أي المنظمة الوطنية العسكرية باللغة العبرية، بقيادة مناحيم بيغين و ليهي. وتُشير سجلات ملكيـة الأراضـي إلـى أن خمسـة وتسـعون بالمائـة (95٪) مـن الأراضـي هـي أملاك لفلسطينيين والباقي بالمائـة (5٪) تعـود ملكيتها لليهـود.

إحصائيات دير ياسين:
ملكية فلسطينية:	2701دونم
ملكية يهوديـة:	153 دونم
ملكية عامـة:	3 دونم
المجمـوع :	2857 دونم

حتــى اليـوم، تبقــى بعـض المنـازل القديمـة فـي لفتـا مهجـورة أو مُدمـرة، ولكـن معظـم المنـازل فـي الحـي الجديـد فـي لفتـا والـذي يمتّـد حتـى شـارع يافـا ومناطـق أخـرى مأهولـة مـن قبـل اليهـود. وتُستخدم مدرسـة القريـة الثانويـة حاليـاً كموقـع دينـي يهـودي. كمـا يقـوم حاليـاً عـدداً مـن مبانـي الفنـادق، مثـل فنـدق سونسـتا وكـراون بـلازا، علـى أراضـي تابعـة لقريـة لفتـا. و الأهـم مـن ذلـك، فـإن معظـم مبانـي الـوزارات الإسرائيليـة، بمـا فـي ذلـك مكتـب رئيـس الـوزراء، ووزارتـي الخارجيـة والداخليـة، والكنيسـت البرلمـان الإسرائيلي قائمـة حاليـاً علـى أراضـي تابعـة لقريـة لفتـا وبلـدة الشـيخ بـدر. فـي الواقـع، فـإن الأرض التـي بُنيـت عليهـا الكنيسـت تعـود ملكيتهـا إلـى عائلـة خلـف الفلسـطينية والتـي يعيـش أفرادهـا اليـوم فـي حـارة الشـيخ جـراح فـي القـدس الشـرقية كـ «غائبيـن حاضريـن.» و لا تـزال هـذه العائلـة تحمـل سـندات ملكيـة هـذه الأرض.

أولاً: قرية لفتـا

قرية لفتا وامتدادها، المعروف ببلدة الشيخ بدر، وجميـع الأراضـي الزراعيـة المحيطـة بمدينـة القـدس من الجهـة الشماليـة:

لقـد تـم إخلاء القريـة وامتدادهـا، المعـروف باسـم بلـدة الشـيخ بـدر، كامـلا بيـن شـهر نيسـان أبريـل وشـهر حزيـران يونيـو مـن العـام 1948، وقـد تـم الإستيلاء علـى جميـع الممتلـكات التـي تركها أهـل القريـة خلفهـم مـن قبـل اليهـود. وفقـا لتعـداد السكـان الـذي أجـري عـام 1945، تُظهـر سـجلات الملكيـة أن تسـعة وثمانـون بالمائـة (89٪) مـن الأراضـي كانـت فلسطينية وأن تسـعة بالمائة (9%) منها يهوديـة وأن بقيـة الأراضـي هـي أراضـي عامـة.

ملاحظة: النسب المئويـة للملكيـة فـي لفتـا وديـر ياسـين وعيـن كارم والمالحـة مأخـوذة مـن «إحصائيـات القـرى» (القـدس: حكومـة فلسطين 1945).

القرى الفلسطينية في القدس الغربية التي تم إخلاء سكانها عام 1948 واستبدالهم باليهود

وأشار الكاتب شهير الس موشيه سميانسكي في مقالة كتبها في صحيفة هآرتس فيذلك الوقت: «لقد تم سرقة بلدات وقرى وممتلكات زراعية دون خجل كما قام أفراد سواء كانوا من الصعاليك من عامة الشعب أو من كبار المثقفين بإثراء أنفسهم من الممتلكات المحتلة؛» (26 يوليو من العام 1948).

وفي ما يلي، نجد وصفاً موجزاً للأحياء الفلسطينية في القدس الغربية وأيضاً للقرى المحيطة بها و التي قد تم إخلاء سكانها عنها في عام 1948، والتي تم إستيلاء على منازلها و على أراضيها لكي يتم أدراجها في حدود بلدية القدس الغربية.

لطالما كانت القدس على طول تاريخها، مدينة موحَّدة. ومنذ القرن السابع وحتى شهر أيار مايو 1948، كانت مدينة عربية فلسطينية تتمتع بحرية الوصول لجميع المؤمنين من الديانات السماوية الثلاث. كما كانت مدينة القدس نموذجاً للتسامح والتعايش، وكانت تُشرف على إدارتها، على مر السنين، بلدية فلسطينية يترأسها على الأغلب رئيس بلدية مسلم.

لقد غيّرت أحداث 1948 و أحداث 1967 هذه الصورة، وذلك عندما قامت قوات يهودية بغزو القدس: فوقع شطرها الغربي، و تلاه بعد ذلك شطرها الشرقي، تحت السيطرة الإسرائيلية المنفردة. وكنتيجة لذلك، فقد قامت القوات الغازية باقتلاع وتهجير السكان الأصليين الفلسطينيين سواء كانوا مسيحيين أو مسلمين، لكي يحل محلهم مُهاجرين يهود بشكلٍ حصري، كما قامت هذه القوات الغازية بتجريدهم من ممتلكاتهم والاستيلاء عليها. و قد كان الهدف من كل ذلك هو التصفية الدائمة لوجود الفلسطينيين الأصليين في القدس، هذا الوجود الذي كان قائماً منذ قرون و توضّح هذه المقالة مرحلتي غزو المدينة المقدسة.

المرحلة الأولى:

ما بعد أيار مايو 1948 - اقتلاع الفلسطينيين من القدس الغربية

حوّلت الأحداث المؤلمة التي جرت بين شهري نيسان أبريل و حزيران يونيو من العام 1948 الـ 60000 ستون ألف فلسطيني الذين طُردوا من منازلهم و من أحيائهم و من قراهم في ما أصبح يُعرف بـ>> القدس اليهودية الغربية << إلى منفيّين واللاجئين دائمين. و أضطر السكان المدنيين على ترك منازلهم بسبب موجة من الهجمات الإرهابية المُتعمَّدة والتي كان تصميمها بهدف تطهير المدينة من غير اليهود تطهيراً عرقياً.

من أفظع هذه الأعمال الشائنة التي ارتكبتها المنظمات الإرهابية اليهودية وأسوءها ٔ هي مجزرة ارتُكبت في التاسع من نيسان أبريل لعام 1948 بحق المدنيين في قرية دير ياسين والتي تقع على مشارف القدس و بالإضافة إلى ذلك فهناك أيضاً حادثة تفجير فندق سميراميس في حي القطمون الفلسطيني.

في شهر أيلول سبتمبر من العام 1948، قامت إسرائيل بالإعلان أن السكان المدنيين الفلسطينيين قد أصبحوا «غائبين دائمين»، كما لم تسمح لهم بالعودة إلى ديارهم وذلك على الرغم من قرار الجمعية العامة للأمم المتحدة رقم 194 والذي يدعو لعودتهم. ونتيجة لذلك، تم إعلان عن جميع ممتلكاتهم كـ «أملاك غائبين» وتم وضعها تحت سلطة ما يسمى بـ «حارس أملاك الغائبين الإسرائيلي.» وفي العام 1950، قام قانون أملاك الغائبين، الذي وقع عليه وزيراً للمالية، بالسماح بمصادرة الممتلكات الفلسطينية، وأعطى ذلك القانون السلطة الكاملة لحارس الأملاك لبيع هذه الأراضي والممتلكات. لقد كان هذا هو «القانون»، إنجاز التعبير، الذي إخترعه اليهود لتنفيذ واحدة من أكبر السرقات للممتلكات من القرن الماضي.

98

الغزو اليهودي للقدس الغربية والشرقية:
من 1948 حتى اليوم

بقلم: إبراهيم مطر

If you enjoyed reading the book by this author,
stay tuned for his second book

About the Author

Ibrahim Matar is a Palestinian economist from Jerusalem. He completed his high school education at the Freres College in the Old City of Jerusalem. He received his BA from the American University of Beirut and a postgraduate degree in development economics from Indiana University, Indiana, USA. He was the previous founder and chairman of the Department of Business and Economics at Bethlehem University. His working career focused on the social and economic development of the West Bank employed by the International Council of Voluntary Agencies such as the Lutheran World Federation (LWF), the Mennonite Central Committee (MCC), and American Near East Refugee Aid (ANERA) and as a senior program officer with the Italian Cooperation Office of the Italian Consulate General in Jerusalem. He has published a number of articles on Jewish settlements and Palestinian rights and peace as well as the Jewish conquest of West and East Jerusalem from 1948 to present.

CPSIA information can be obtained
at www.ICGtesting.com
Printed in the USA
LVHW070758230822
726633LV00010B/167